The United States Consul-General

Labor and Porcelain in Japan

The United States Consul-General

Labor and Porcelain in Japan

ISBN/EAN: 9783337173166

Printed in Europe, USA, Canada, Australia, Japan

Cover: Foto ©Suzi / pixelio.de

More available books at **www.hansebooks.com**

LABOR AND PORCELAIN

IN JAPAN.

BY

THE UNITED STATES CONSUL-GENERAL.

ILLUSTRATED.

———◦———

YOKOHAMA:
PRINTED AT THE "JAPAN GAZETTE" OFFICE, 70, MAIN STREET.
—•—
1882.

HIS IMPERIAL MAJESTY
MUTSU HITO,
EMPEROR OF JAPAN.

HER IMPERIAL MAJESTY
HARUKO,
EMPRESS OF JAPAN.

INDEX

TO REPORT ON LABOR IN JAPAN.

INDEX

TO REPORT ON THE POTTERY AND PORCELAIN INDUSTRIES IN JAPAN.

LABOR IN JAPAN.

——∘o⦂⦂o∘——

REPORT

BY

CONSUL-GENERAL VAN BUREN,

ON THE

Topography, Soil, Climate, Laws, Religion, Government,
Education, The Prices of Labor, Living, &c.,

OF JAPAN.*

IN all historic times the subject of labor and the
condition of the laborer have been of the first
importance. In later ages, since trade and commerce
have multiplied population, increased wealth, and ac-
cumulated capital in a few hands, the question has been
complicated by that of the relations which should exist
between capital and labor; and now that steam · and
electricity are bringing all nationalities and races into
close and active competition, the subject has received
added importance.

---

* Reprinted from *Reports from the Consuls of the United States.*
No. 2.—November, 1880. Published by the department of state,
according to act of congress.

In all the countries of the civilized world this topic is agitating the public mind, and is being discussed in the halls of legislation, in the busy marts of trade, on the great money changes, in the homes of the artisans, and in the huts and hovels of the humblest toilers. All systems of government and all organizations of society on every continent and on the far-off islands of the ocean are disturbed by this question and its portending conflict.

In view of this a full, accurate, and comprehensive account of the condition of the laborers of any race or country is of more than passing importance. The following statement of the status of labor in a new and comparatively unknown land cannot fail, therefore, to be of interest.

It is now nearly a quarter of a century since Perry opened the sealed gateways of Japan to the commerce and travel of the world. The unique civilization of an island empire, with an area of 150,000 square miles and more than 35,000,000 of people, was then first presented to modern times for study and investigation. Since that libraries of books and pamphlets, and volumes of letters have been written upon every phase of that civilization, except the status and condition of the laborer. Of the importance and power of 35,000,000 of people as added factors in the products of the world there can be no question.

In this paper I shall refer briefly to all facts that seem to me to affect to any appreciable extent the condition of the laboring population of Japan, believing that such information will be found valuable to the economist, statesman, or philanthropist, who shall make the happiness of mankind his study. The topography, soil, climate, laws, religion, government, education, morals, finances, and means of transportation, as well as the prices of labor and living, all have an influence, directly or indirectly, upon the condition of the laborer, and are all, therefore, legitimate subjects of study in this connection.

.LATITUDE AND LONGITUDE OF JAPAN.

The islands of Japan extend along the eastern coast of Asia, from the 31st to the 49th parallels of north latitude, and from the 130th to the 145 degrees of east longitude. It is estimated that these islands contain from 150,000 to 160,000 square miles, or once and a half the area of the British Isles.

TOPOGRAPHY.

Through the centre of this island chain is one long mountain range, with spurs of lesser elevation running at right angles. Interspersed through all these mountain masses are innumerable fertile valleys, through which the drainage of the whole area finds its way to the sea. Along either coast are extensive alluvial plains, the weatherings and washings of the mountains during untold centuries. The crests of the higher mountains are rocky and precipitous but as the spurs slope away toward the sea they present gentler hill-sides susceptible of tillage. It is on these alluvial plains along the sea, through these fertile valleys, and on the gentle mountain slopes, that the laborer is to be found. Both the eastern and western coasts present deep indentations of gulfs and bays extending far into the mainland.

SOIL.

For all the purposes of this paper, it is sufficient to say that the soil with which the laborer of Japan has to deal, is a black, vegetable mould, from 2 to 10 feet in depth, superimposed upon a deep clay subsoil. This mould is a mass of decomposed vegetation, grown luxuriantly in a warm summer climate, combined with a great rainfall. It is a true humus, with an excess of humic acid, which renders its fertile elements more or less insoluble. Even in its virgin state this black, rich-looking soil, without some chemical solvent, will not produce a paying crop, but with lime or potash every product of the latitude grows luxuriantly.

WATER.

Draining the great mountain range and its spurs is a system of rivers and canals, furnishing abundance of clear, pure water. Excellent wells can be had almost everywhere on the lower levels, for the digging.

CLIMATE.

I shall not attempt to give the full meteorology of this country, as the temperature and rainfall will be sufficient for our purposes.

Temperature.—In Yokohama, in latitude 35 degrees 46.minutes observations have been made for nine years. The following are the monthly and annual means of temperature :—

	Fhar.		Fahr.
January	39.2	July	78.7
February	42.2	August	79.4
March	46.0	September	70.2
April	54.7	October	59.8
May	64.6	November	49.5
June	71.6	December	47.5

Annual mean 57.7

The highest temperature for these nine years was 93 degrees, the lowest, 21 degrees. The absolute range of mercury was, therefore, 72 degrees.

Rainfall.—The average precipitation, as observed at the same place and for about the same time, was as follows :—

	Inches.		Inches.
January	4.23	July	3.15
February	4.22	August	6.62
March	3.19	September	12.05
April	5.84	October	6.14
May	4.33	November	8.67
June	10.17	December	2.56

Annual rainfall 71.17

The greatest amount of snow which has fallen at Yokohama for one year is 15 inches. The highest annual precipitation since foreign trade with this country was in 1868, being 122 inches, and the smallest amount in 1867, being 42 inches.

The following table shows the average number of rainy days for each month in the years :—

January	4.42	July	10.00
February	6.28	August	9.28
March	8.42	September	11.85
April	9.72	October	7.00
May	8.42	November	6.57
June	11.28	December	4.28

Average rainy days per year 97.52

POPULATION.

The population of Japan as shown by the census of 1878, is between 35,000,000 and 36,000,000 but as full tables of that census are not as yet available, I have been compelled to resort to those of the census of two years earlier. The population at that time was 33,300,675.

Number of the higher and lower nobility 1,894,784
Common people 31,405,891
Number of males of whole population 16,891,729
Number of females of whole population 16,408,946

Number of farmers, males 8,004,014
Number of farmers, females 6,866,412
                                                      14,870,426
Number of mechanics, males 521,295
Number of mechanics, females 180,121
                                                      701,416
Number of merchants, males 819,782
Number of merchants, females 489,409
                                                      1,309,191
Mixed occupations, males 1,218,266
Mixed occupations, females 911,256
                                                      2,129,522

Total producing population 19,010,555

Of children under fourteen years of age there were 9,056,309

AINOS.

GOVERNMENT.

The Government of Japan up to 1868 was absolute and irresponsible, with an emperor at its head who held all authority by divine right, and who ruled through a number of feudal princes, at whose head, stood the Shogun (Tycoon).

The laborer had no privileges, except such as his immediate prince conceded. He was absolutely under the control and in the power of his feudal lord, and that lord's retainers.

There were no courts for the trial of causes which might arise between him and his superiors. The position of the laborer was so immeasurably below that of the ruling class that it was as much as his life and liberty were worth to even petition his prince or appeal to the Shogun or Emperor against any act of the upper classes. The common people were bound to the soil, and could not leave it without permission. Their lives even were in the hands of their immediate superiors, and fancied insolence or insubordination was sufficient justification for taking them. The government divided the people into five general classes, as follows :—

1. Military and official : this class included the Emperor and his blue-blooded nobility, the Tycoon and Daimios, and their retainers.

2. Farmers who held land under lease.

3. Artisans.

4. Merchants and bankers.

5. Laborers, or the coolie class.

There was the widest gulf between the first class and all the others. The latter had no rights which the first class were bound to respect.

In 1868 the government was essentially remodeled. The feudal system was abolished; the feudal lords were pensioned, and their power taken from them and assumed by the central government.

Although the laborer has no voice in the making and execution of the laws, he has been materially benefited by the change. A system of courts has been established, wherein he can be heard against even the highest classes. He can claim the intervention of these courts to insure the payment of his wages, which he could not do under the old organization.

A vast, burdensome system of men-at-arms, with absolute authority, has been set aside, the old divisions of the people abolished, and all, in the eye of the law, made of the same class. Of course, the power and influence of the old class system is still felt, and will be for years; but it must gradually die out, and thus the laborer will be on equal ground with all. One peculiar feature of the old absolutism, however, still exists. I refer to the police surveillance of all the people. The empire is divided into districts, called ken and fu, over each of which is placed an officer, known as the "ken-rei," or "fu-chiji," rendered in English, "governor." At the office of this official every native resident must be registered, and he or she cannot remove to another ken without written permission first obtained; and upon arrival at destination, he or she must be immediately registered there. And so strict is this supervision that a Japanese cannot travel, or even sleep, out of his district without permission of the authorities. A block of every ten houses has its supervising officer, and each hundred a superior official, keeping watch and ward over the movements of the occupants, so that any change or movement, even for a day, is immediately known. And this interference by the government is not confined to the movements of the people, but extends to all their trades and industries. Monopolies are granted to certain parties, either of trade or transportation, and the government itself often becomes a purchaser and seller in the market.

LAND TENURE.

All the land of the empire was the Emperor's. Through the Shogun (Tycoon) it was granted to military favorites for the maintenance of the military power. These favorites leased it in small divisions to farmers, who held it at the pleasure of the lessors. So long as the lessee paid the stipulated price, in produce, he was left undisturbed. Such was the land tenure up to 1868. Since that time the feudal institutions have been abolished, the land tenure has been changed, and the land has been sold, and is held in fee simple. This great reform has infinitely bettered the condition of the farmer. About three-tenths of all tilled land is now in the possession of small proprietors, the balance being held in larger divisions.

ORGANIZATION OF DOMESTIC SOCIETY.

Society was here, as elsewhere in Asia, essentially patriarchal. The pater-familias had almost unlimited control over all the members of the family. The whole course of life of a child was marked out, shaped, and controlled by the father. Marriages were entirely within his authority. No son or daughter, no matter of what age, could leave the paternal roof and go out into the world without the parental consent. Among the lower classes, daughters were sold by their parents to be concubines, or to be trained as singing girls, or for immoral purposes, or they were mortgaged for a term of years to labor.

When a girl left the house of her parents and entered another as a wife or concubine, all the allegiance due to her parents was transferred to her husband, or master, and his parents. She could be divorced and sent away from her children, at the will of the husband and his family.

Much of this power of the pater-familias has been done away with, but his authority is still incomparably greater than in any Western society.

RELIGION.

The religion of the imperial families is Shintoism, or the worship of the country or empire through its heroes or great men. That of the great mass of people is Buddhism; not that of India, but a system grafted upon the original Pagan worship, and retaining much of the gross superstitions of the latter.

The common people not only believe in the Budd-histic deities, but also in the demons and evil spirits of Paganism. These religious beliefs and superstitions affect directly the condition of the laboring classes. The belief in *shrine cure* prevails everywhere with them. The result is a large number of blind and diseased persons, who, if they had been properly medicated in time, would be healthy producers instead of burdens upon society. Large numbers of children, when sick, are carried to the favorite shrine instead of to the doctor, and thus mortality and the number of physically weak and diseased people are largely increased.

The priesthood, although less than formerly, is still a mighty power with the lower classes, and the income of shrines and temples, although materially reduced, is still immense and a most oppressive burden to the people.

EDUCATION.

The education of the higher classes was in former times Chinese. The literature, philosophy, and science (if it can be said that there was any true science) were all Chinese. It is safe to say that among these higher classes there was no illiteracy ; all could read and write. Nearly all of the other classes, although not learned, could also read and write enough for their business purposes. There were, of course, exceptions, but of the male farmers and artisans not ten per cent. were illiterate. Schools were to be found in the large towns of the provinces and in many of the smaller villages.

Where schools were not available, reading and writing were, in some measure taught in the household.

It must be understood that what is denominated as education here is not education in the sense the term is used in Europe and America, and especially in recent times. The most highly educated man in Japan knew some thousands of Chinese characters, a few books of the Chinese classics, the books of ceremonies, and some of the truisms and proverbs of the Chinese sages, and could write impromptu poetry in Chinese characters. He need not know the history even of his own country, much less than of any other. He had absolutely no knowledge of anything worthy the name of science. In art, he might paint and draw,

The lower classes, in place of this Chinese culture, knew just enough arithmetic to serve their daily use and could read and write in the Japanese characters. There was some knowledge of Japanese history, mixed up with the marvellous, gleaned from books or the travelling story-teller, who, by the roadside, recited to gaping crowds the stories of the wars and amours of the olden times.

The whole system of education has been remodelled since 1868. Public schools have been established and scientific text-books from Europe and America have been translated and brought into use. Probably the percentage of illiteracy has not been much reduced by these reforms, but the scientific learning of the West has largely taken the place of the useless proverbs and superstitions of the East. It is safe to say that, at the present rate of educational progress, another decade will see a useful education within reach of every Japanese laborer.

The report of the Minister of Education for the year 1879 shows :—

Number of elementary schools	25,459
Number of teachers	59,825
School population	5,251,807
Scholars	2,066,566

The per cent. of scholars to school population, therefore, seems to be about 39.3. There are 389 schools of a higher grade with 910 teachers and 20,522 scholars. There are 96 normal schools with 766 teachers and 7,949 scholars. There exist also two so-called universities.

The whole amount of school expenditure, as shown in said report, was 5,364,870 yen,* of which 2,640,629 yen were paid in salaries, the salary of each teacher being an average of 44.72 yen per year.

Public libraries have been opened, one of which, at Tokio, has about 70,000 volumes.

Medical science and education.—The health and welfare of the laborer and his family everywhere, are largely affected by the system of medicine prevailing, and by the intelligence of the members of the profession. An intelligent system of medicine, a high standard of admission to its practice, with low fees, give a lower percentage of mortality, a higher physique and fewer lame, blind, and deaf.

* The Japanese yen=$0.99·7.

The first system of medicine that, in any degree, took the place of *shrine cure*, was the Chinese, which had no claims to be a science, and was full of ignorance, superstitions, and absurdities. The system had no knowledge of anatomy, physiology, pathology, chemistry, or the properties or actions of medicines. This was, and is the old school of medicine in Japan. Upon it was built a new system by the introduction of Dutch medical text-books, in the seven-teenth century, which struggled for supremacy with the Chinese school for two hundred years.

Although this was an improvement upon the old practice, the latter continued to embrace the most numerous followers and to receive the confidence of the laboring classes, whenever they emancipated themselves from the superstitions of the shrine cures of the priesthood.

When the country was opened to foreign intercourse, modern medicine was introduced. Within the past ten years a medical college has been established in Tokio, and all the local or ken governments have opened hospitals, with a foreign surgeon for each, and a class of medical students.

These local schools were necessarily inefficient, as no one man is fitted, or has the time to teach all the branches of medicine and surgery, but with the text-books and the clinics of the hospital, a better class of practitioners than the country has ever had before has been sent out. I know of no means of arriving at the number of practitioners of these several schools in the whole empire.

A Samurai in Armor.

In this ken or province of Kanagawa, in which this consulate-general at Yokohama is situated, there are 659 practicing physicians; of these, 41 are students of the new schools and hospitals, 106 of the old Dutch school, and 521 of the Chinese school.

The population of this ken is now (1880) about 500,000. This gives one physician to 760 people. It must be borne in mind that this ken contains the principal foreign port and has had a hospital for years, with a foreign surgeon, and is within 20 miles of the medical college in Tokio. In the interior, I do not think there is more than one physician to every 1,500 people, and the old, ignorant Chinese method preponderates more largely than here.

MORALS.

It is difficult to write of the morals of the Japanese people in such manner as to make the subject entirely intelligible to the Western reader. The habits and customs of centuries in which the relations of the sexes in this country have been looked upon so differently to those to which we have been accustomed, have created a code of morals, if the term be permissible, from which morality, in this connection, has been excluded. The relation of master and concubine is here considered perfectly proper, and neither party loses caste or respectability. Respectable parents sell their daughters for this purpose, and even to become inmates of houses of prostitution. From these latter places it not infrequently occurs that girls are taken to become excellent wives and mothers.

After marriage, the wife is expected to be true to her husband, and it seldom happens that she fails in this duty. As mothers, Japanese women are models. None can be kinder or more affectionate to their children than they. They will spare no pains to amuse or instruct them, and seldom use force to compel obedience or punish faults. As wives, these women are simply slaves to the humors and caprices of their husbands and the families of their husbands. They have absolutely no rights, and are often subjected to seeing the attentions of their lords transfered to some favorite concubine, to whom they are obliged to be considerate and respectful.

Bathing together, by both sexes, in public bath-houses, in a state of nudity, is practiced everywhere, but rudeness, vulgar language, or indecent gestures, in these places, are never indulged in.

As has been seen in the statistics of population, the males in Japan greatly exceed in number the females, and, in consequence of this fact, and the additional one of concubinage, so largely practiced, the number of unmarried men among the labouring class, is very large. These persons frequent houses of prostitution, and spend much of their earnings also in gambling and drinking. It must be said, however, that drunkenness is exceptional, especially among the better class of laborers.

The strong drink is "saké," a distilled spirit made mostly from rice, of about the strength of ordinary table sherry.

The Japanese, like all Eastern people, are somewhat
given to exaggeration in their speech and their intense
sauvity and politeness to each other are proverbial.

MEANS OF TRANSPORTATION.

The islands of Japan are long and narrow. There
is no point in the centre of the larger island more than
100 miles, from navigable water. Cheap oceanic transportation is therefore, everywhere easily available. On
the alluvial plains of the eastern and western coasts,
besides the tidal rivers, there exists an extensive system
of canals. In the interior, in former times, there was
no general system of roads worthy of the name. It is
true, the Tokugawa Tycoons, and some of the Daimios
had built a few roads, but they were ill adapted to
carriage traffic, and in places, were entirely impassable
except for footmen and packhorses. Aside from these
roads, built for purposes of war the only means of travel
were mere footpaths.

Now two short lines of railway have been built, in all
less than 100 miles. Some of the footpaths have been
made wide enough for carriages, but, in the whole of
Japan, it is safe to say that there are not more than
1,000 miles of carriage roads. From and to the interior
districts, all the products and all articles of trade are
carried on the backs of men or horses. Such carriage
is slow and costly, and ruinous to both producer and
consumer. As a tax, it bears heavily on the shoulders
of labor, and will do so until better roads are built by
the government. So much man-packing is not only

laborious, but degrading. It prevents production, consumption, and trade.

The building of good roads and the providing of cheap transportation must be conditions precedent to the settlement and development of the wild lands of the country.

By sea, river, and canal the means of transportation are reasonably good and cheap. Lines of steamers and sailing vessels, of foreign construction, have been established to all the principal ports of the country. The fleet of vessels owned by one company, the Mitsu-Bishi, represents, in round numbers, a gross tonnage of 50,000 tons. This company has had the countenance and support of the government; its fleet is being constantly increased and the service rendered more effective.

In addition, there are many smaller companies in Tokio, Osaka, and Nagasaki, which run steamers and sailing vessels, of foreign style, to some of the smaller ports. Some of these steamers are Japanese built, and although not of the best construction give promise that in time Japan will be independent of foreign countries in ship-building.

There are no means available for giving accurate data as to the number and tonnage of the old style of native sailing vessels, known as "junks." The gross tonnage must be very large. They run along the coast to and from all the ports, and give cheap service, much cheaper than steam or foreign sailing vessels.

Latterly, loud complaints have been made of the interference by the government with these vessels in the interests of the steam monopolies. Experience will certainly compel an abandonment of such attempts, which, if persisted in, must disastrously affect both the government and people.

As bearing upon the question of inland transportation of the products of labor, the statistics of the number of cattle and horses of both Japan and the United States may be properly inserted here, so that the contrast may be seen.

In Japan, her 35,000,000 people have 900,274 horses and 814,324 cattle. In the United States, in 1870, the 38,000,000 people had, in round numbers, 10,000,000 horses and mules, and 26,000,000 cattle. This will show what burdens the laborer here has to carry on his back, and what unnecessary calls are made upon his earnings in the way of carrying his products.

Mails.—The mail transportation that has been established within the last ten years, both coastwise and inland, is cheap and excellent. The number of miles of mail routes aggregates 36,052. The number of post offices is 3,927. The number of letters carried for the year ending June 30th, 1880, was 55,775,206, and that of newspapers 11,203,731. These figures throw great light upon the volume of business of the country and the amount of reading and writing done by the people.

Connected with the postal department is a well organized postal money-order service and postal savings-bank system. The number of these banks is 595.

TENEMENTS.

In forming an opinion of the tenements of the laborer, the climate of the country must be borne in mind. Although there are unlimited quantities of good, durable building-stone everywhere in the mountain ranges, and vast deposits of firm clay for making brick, no stone or brick houses are built. The frequency and severity of earthquakes make the use of any but wooden structures impracticable. Timber is scarce, and there is nothing worthy the name of forests except in a portion of Yesso, in the far north.

All buildings, or nearly all, are one story and, compared to those of America and Europe, small. But the reader must bear in mind that the requirements of this oriental civilization are less than with us. A laborer's house will, at most, have no more than four little rooms. Generally there is one main room, which serves as a sitting, dining, and sleeping room, and, in addition, a small nook for cooking and another for bathing. That the uses of one room for the purposes of eating, sitting, and sleeping, may be understood, it should be explained that the rooms are covered with clean soft mats, upon which no boot or shoe ever treads. When meals are served, small tables, not more than one foot high, are used, and the family sit on the floor like tailors on their benches. When the meal is finished the table is removed and the room is ready for a sitting-room, the mats serving as seats. At night cotton comforters are brought from a small clothes press and spread on the mats, and lo! a sleeping chamber.

BETTO.

Thus, much of the room required by a laborer of our Western civilization is saved. A Japanese laborer's house with three rooms can be built for from 25 to 100 yen. And the furniture, including matting and sliding partitions, will not exceed 50 yen.

The house, by reason of non-use by the people of boots and shoes, is neat and clean. The bath, found in almost every laborer's house, is in daily use, and, cheap and small as the house is, it is comfortable.

None of the houses are built with a view to ventilation or warmth, the partitions and sides being of paper, protected in cold weather or storms by strong wooden shutters. The vast majority of the houses are thatched, and therefore stove-pipes and chimneys are impossible. In fact, there are no stoves or grates in Japan. In villages and towns the house is warmed, if at all, by a small fire-box filled with charcoal, but more generally by a square zinc or copper lined fire-place, sunk in the middle of the floor, in which wood is burned, the smoke from which rises and escapes through a hole in the roof. But little heat is generated in this way, and much discomfort from the smoke is experienced, and diseases of the eye are prevalent.

As a rule, the principal protection from cold is by additional padded clothing. The laborer, however, suffers in the three winter months, when, although in many parts of the empire the thermometer does not mark very low, the cold storms of snow and rain are exceedingly uncomfortable,

The drainage from sinks and cess-pools in the vicinity of tenements is, as a rule, extremely defective, and is, doubtless, a powerful agent in producing epidemic disease.

In 1875, when the population was 33,300,675, there were 7,389,371 houses or tenements, the average number of occupants to each being, therefore, less than 5. In Tokio the number is 4; in Kanagawa ken, 4.5; Nagasaki ken, 4.7; Fukushima ken, 5.5; Miyagi ken, 5.9; Awomori ken, 5.8; Osaka City, 3.7.

The houses of cities seem to be less crowded than those of the poorer rural districts.

FUEL.

The fuel, which is used chiefly for cooking and heating baths, is charcoal, cut and split wood, brush and dried grass.

Charcoal is made in the wooded regions, burned in small clay pits, and carried to the settlements on the backs of men and horses in straw sacks. The selling price varies according to the distance from which it is brought, from 25 to 50 cents per 100 pounds. Cut wood is sold in small bundles of six sticks, each stick being about 18 inches in length, and 2 inches in diameter; 80 to 100 bundles are sold for $1. I am quoting the rates of districts remote from the foreign settlements.

Brush and dried grass are gathered from the wild lands, to which certain rights of commons attach, as in England in early times. The value of the fuel bought and sold in 1875 was as follows: Wood, $6,107,974; Charcoal, $2,219,986.

As the farmer and country laborer gets his fuel from his own land or from the commons, this must have been mostly used in the larger villages and cities, showing how little is consumed for house warming even by the richer classes.

FARMERS.

As has been said, the farmer, under the old system of classes, ranked next to the samurai or governing class. In the new order he holds the same position in public opinion and general estimation. He is now owner of the soil he tills, and is taxed according to its producing capacity.

The kocho, or village officer, in all agricultural villages, has always been a leading farmer, and some villages had and still have the right to choose this officer. He had little more than a general supervision of village affairs. He settled petty disputes, maintained the peace, kept the register of the inhabitants, granted travelling permits, arrested thieves, and was a general advisor for the village.

Within the past two years the government has taken a step which has greatly enhanced the position and influence of the landholder. A decree has been promulgated by which local elective assemblies have been created, the electors of which are confined to such of the landholders as pay at least $10 land tax.

At present the power of these assemblies is only deliberative and advisory. The governor of the province submits his fiscal estimates for local expenditures and they examine and pass upon them. If they disagree with him the whole matter goes to the general government for its decision.

Although these assemblies possess no legislative power, they contain the germ of representative local self-government. The system needs to be extended so as to include, among the representatives, intelligent people of all classes, and to have the power now exercised materially increased. That this consummation will be achieved is almost certain. Nor will reform in this direction stop here.

The agitation pervading all classes in Japan in favor of a national representative assembly is manifested daily in petitions to the Emperor and his ministers, in conferences and lectures, and in newspaper communications and editorials. The question is so prominent and the determination to achieve success so universal, that the Genro-in, the deliberative and advisory council of the Empire is now said to be taking it into serious consideration, and probably the country, before the lapse of many years, possibly months, will find itself in possession of some such chamber, wherein the views of all the people may be presented and discussed, and laws for their welfare enacted. That it will be entirely free to act as its members may be inclined is not probable, and it may be matter of doubt if such freedom would at present be wise.

Farmers in Japan have no seasons of rest as in colder climates, the climate in nearly all portions of the country being so mild in winter as to admit of raising the hardier crops.

A considerable percentage of the land-owners are not workers, large numbers of the tea, silk, rice, tobacco, and sugar raisers being able to employ laborers for that purpose.

Almost every farmer can read, write, and keep his farm accounts. He sends his sons to some school to learn the same, and has his daughters taught music and needle work at home.

All labor on a farm is, to the present time, mere hand work. A plow is seldom seen. Sometimes in the lowland rice-fields an implement 5 feet in length with a wooden cross-piece and depending iron teeth 20 inches in length, set 4 or 5 inches apart, is used with a horse as a pulverizer of the soil after the latter has been thoroughly dug up and worked over with a mattock. Ninety-nine per cent., however, of all labor is still manual. In 1878 the number of farmers, out of a population of 35,000,000, was something over 15,500,000, of which over 7,000,000 were women ; but as a large number of these latter, including the old and young, are engaged in household duties, spinning, weaving, making clothing, &c., there were probably not more than two or three millions of women employed in field work.

The area of land in actual cultivation in the whole empire in 1875 was about 12,000,000 acres, so that to the actual farming population there were only three-quarters of an acre per head. The tillage is of the most thorough order. Two crops are invariably raised each year, so that the producing capacity of the area cultivated is double that of the number of acres named.

The wages of an able-bodied farm-hand are about $35 per year with board, and without board, $50. Per day, with board, it will not average more than 15 to 20 cents. Female labor is much cheaper. To do work in a house or on a farm stout healthy women are engaged at from $8 to $10 per year with food, and without food $25 to $30, and by the day at from 10 to 15 cents. The number of hours of labor will not average more than 9 and probably not more than 8.

The Japanese farmer is an easy task-master, and treats his hired laborer with great kindness. In ordinary farming there is little skilled labor, but in tea, silk, and sugar cultivation and preparation, skill and experience are required, and are paid higher prices. A good tea-firer on a tea plantation, or a silk winder, receives double the wages of the unskilled laborer.

Food.—The food of a farm-laborer is almost entirely vegetable. It consists of rice, barley, or wheat, millet, beans, pease, turnips, potatoes, onions, carrots, and a few other vegetable products. In some districts rice is too high in price, and only barley, turnips, and millet, with some few additions, are used. On rare occasions the laborer may eat an egg or chicken and some cheap fish, but he is essentially a vegetarian. Religion, custom, popular prejudice, and price forbid the use of animal flesh.

Clothing.—The clothing of the farm-laborer in summer is little more than nature sent him into the world with; in winter, a cotton garment or two is worn, with

straw sandals or wooden clogs. The whole clothing of
a year will not cost more than $4 or $5.

Holidays.—Several holidays are allowed each year,
such as religious festivals and family celebrations.
When a man and his wife work for yearly wages they
will receive, without board, about $75. From this he
has to pay from $8 to $10 for a two or three small-
roomed house, and buy clothing for a family of four or
five amounting, perhaps, to $20. He will have a small
garden with his house, from which one-half of his living
is produced; a few chickens and ducks, tended by the
children, will buy many articles of necessity for holiday
use; a child of six or seven years, perhaps with a babe
of six months strapped on its back, will gather brush or
dried grass on the commons for fuel; and by great
frugality in eating, and scrupulous care of clothing, at
the end of a year he finds he has supported his family,
had several enjoyable holidays, and has a few dollars
hidden away in some secret place.

Taxes.*—The average government tax of low irrigable
rice-land is $5 per acre. The average value of such
lands is $200 per acre. The land tax is therefore 2½
per cent.; this is the government assessment; that for
local purposes is ½ per cent., making 3 per cent. in all.

Rice Culture.—The average value of the product of
rice-land is about $40 per acre. Four or five acres of
lowland rice-fields form quite a respectable holding for
one person. This, with another acre or so of upland

---

* As to general taxation, see table B.

where vegetables are raised, and a little bluff land for
timber, fuel, and grass to feed the pack-horse, supports
his family, pays for hired help, and gives a little surplus
at the annual settling day.

The homes of the rice, silk, and tea farmers are the
best of all the agricultural laborers in Japan. The
house is often as large as 30 or 40 feet square, universally one story, thatched roof, strongly built, with
verandah in front, and five or six rooms, one being kept
as a spare or reception room. If built with a view to
light and warmth, they would compare in comfort with
the average New England farm-house.

Rice.—Rice is grown in all the sixty provinces of
Japan. The whole area in cultivation in 1878 was about
6,500,000 acres, and the product was 180,000,000
bushels. This includes upland as well as lowland rice,
the average yield of all being about 30 bushels per acre.
On low land the yield will average 40 bushels.

The total value of the rice product, as returned to
the home department in 1878, was $202,521,750.

Wheat.—Wheat is grown in all parts of the empire.
The product in 1878 was 38,000,000 bushels, valued at
$19,000,000.

Barley.—The climate and soil are everywhere favor-
able to the growth of barley. The product in 1878 was
60,000,000 bushels, valued at $36,000,000.

Millet, Beans, Peas, &c.—The value of these products
for the same year was returned as $16,007,360.

The value of all other vegetables was $10,849,628,
and of seeds and fruits $8,217,798.

GEISHA, PLAYING ON THE TSUDZUMI.

Tobacco.—The product of tobacco was about 90,000,000 pounds, valued at $7,500,000. A considerable quantity was exported to England and Germany. The quantity is inferior and the price low, but much higher than ten years ago, averaging about 8½ cents per pound.

Tea.—The tea-culture is one of the most important and lucrative of all Japanese industries, the leaf being one of the chief articles of export. The product in 1878 was about 60,000,000 pounds. The export trade has increased wonderfully. In 1869 the amount exported was 4,890,430 pounds; in 1875, 22,384,893 pounds; in 1879, 33,692,391 pounds; and that of 1880 is estimated to reach 38,000,000 pounds.

As has been remarked, the tea farmer lives in a comparatively good house, has servants, keeps a horse to do his packing, and has a balance to his credit at the end of a good year.

The best tea grows on the hillsides, sheltered from the sea-winds, which latter make the leaf tought and of bad flavor.

The ordinary labor wages are paid for the tillage of the soil, but the man who trims the plant must be skilled, and will get as high as 30 to 35 cents per day. The tea-picking is done by women and girls and requires care. When they work by the day they get from 10 to 12½ cents. Tea rollers and firers in the country must be skilled, and they command from 15 to 30 cents per day. In the open ports tea-firing is done entirely by women, who are paid about 15 cents per day.

In the export of tea there is employment for a large number of carpenters in making boxes, printers and lithographers in the manufacture of labels, &c., who are paid as skilled mechanics.

The area of tea-growing is rapidly increasing and as there are plenty of hillsides and plains well adapted for the culture available and still unoccupied, it will increase as long as there is a foreign demand. It seems to be one of the great fields for the spread and use of an increasing labor population. The habit of adulterating tea, however, with leaves of the wisteria seems to be on the increase in this country, and if not arrested may materially affect the demand. The wisteria leaf is not poisonous, but cannot be said to improve the flavor of the cup that " cheers, but not inebriates."

Silk.--The area of land in mulberry trees is not stated in any of the late census product returns. In 1875 the total value of silk product is given at $31,250,000 The export of silk and silk worm eggs for the year ending June 30th, 1878, was $11,640,976.64.

The trade is steadily growing and giving increasing employment to labor, and, as better processes of preparing silk are introduced and a better article is produced, more and more skilled labor will be required and higher wages be paid.

Mulberry plantations are found in fifty of the sixty-six provinces of Japan. The soil nowhere is exclusively devoted to this tree. Universally between the rows of trees, other crops, both summer and winter, are grown. The business of silk production is carried on in the house where the family lives. The mulberry leaves are either picked off by women and children and carried into the house, or the young limbs with the leaves on are cut off and taken there, where the leaves are picked off, washed, cup up, and fed to the worms. Little skill is required.

When the cocoons are ready for winding, that, as well as the other work thus far referred to, is done by women and girls. To make an even thread requires experience, care, and skill, and such labor commands wages accordingly. Spinning, warping, dyeing, and weaving are all more or less skilled branches and require skilled labor.

There are some establishments that buy the cocoons, wind them, spin the thread, and weave the cloth ; but nine-tenths of the silk, raw and manufactured, of the country is family made. The machinery of manufacture, whether in the factory or private house, is crude, and still remains as though Jacquard and Arkwright never lived. The beautiful stuffs made by such crude means testify to their skill and ingenuity.

The man who tends the trees commands ordinary farm wages, while the leaf-pickers and feeders, spinners, and weavers of plain cloth will get from 20 to 40 cents per day. Weavers of fancy-patterned goods get much more, even as high as $1 per day; but this is very exceptional.

Cotton.—Reliable statistics cannot be obtained by which to estimate the amount of this staple raised in the country. The returns of 1875 show cotton goods manufactured to the value of $10,564,578, and that it formed part of textures valued at $12,915,586. The cotton itself is coarse, and in consequence the manufactured cloth is of an inferior quality, and the labor employed is no not skilled and commands small wages. It is generally believed that these manufacturers have increased within the past few years from 30 to 40 per cent.

ARTISANS.

The Japanese artisan, like the farmer, has always held a respectable position. He was in a class above the merchant and banker, but in reality his position, pay, and privileges were no greater.

For a thousand years a very high mechanical art has existed. The Japanese articles and implements of steel were of the best. Some of the old swords are worthy to be classed with the Toledo and Damascus blades. Their lacquered wares have been and still are unrivalled, and they made beautiful porcelain long before Palissy and Böttcher were born. Their silk cloth, embroideries, and silk tapestries were exquisitely beautiful at a time when some western peoples wore the coarsest stuffs. Their oldest bronze compares with the finest products of Europe. Their paintings on silk and paper, porcelain and lacquer, excite the warmest admiration. Their ivory and wood carvings are wonders of skill, ingenuity, and patient labor.

There is hardly a house in Japan where some mechanical trade is not carried on. Even in the households of the higher classes, silk, cotton, and other goods are made by the servants, and the members of the family have some knowledge of the art. Every farmer's house has its wheel and loom. Many of the smaller merchants make more or less of their goods.

In this view there are many more artisans in the country than are shown by the census of 1875. The number, as I have previously stated, is placed between 700,000 and 800,000. I believe that there are more than double that number who devote the greater share of their time to manufacture, and five or six millions who work more or less at mechanical trades.

Many of the wares used for home consumption require no special skill in their production, and therefore the labor wage is low. In the manufacture of silk. lacquer, porcelain, enamels, bronzes, embroideries, and in their paintings, skilled labor must enter, and is paid proportionately.

What has been said of agricultural labor as to the use of machinery, can be repeated of mechanical work, It is, in the main, hand labor. Labor-saving machinery does not enter as a factor, to any appreciable extent, into the industries of Japan. I doubt if there are more than two sawmills in the whole empire. All such labor is by hand in every branch of mechanical art.

Porcelain and Earthenware.—Porcelain and earthenware are manufactured in every province. By the last census returns available (1875) the value of all porcelain produced was about $3,000,000. With one exception, that of the home department in the province of Hizen, there is no foreign machinery or mode of manufacture in use. The clay is manipulated as it was in the earliest days. The same wheel is used for turning that is pictured on the walls of the tombs and temples of Egypt. All decorations are by hand. There is a marked improvement of late years in designs and decorations of all kinds of articles of ornament. No more beautiful or exquisite, ceramic articles are made than come from the hands of the Japanese artisan. Love of beautiful pottery has been a national passion for a thousand years, and skilled labor has commanded relatively high wages.

Much of the cruder work can be done by apprentices and common journeymen, but a good turner at the wheel gets 50 to 70 cents per day, and the best painters from 75 cents to $1.15. The average is, however, much less.

Makers of flowers and figures of birds, &c., for ornamenting the larger vases and jars in bas-relief receive from 50 to 70 cents per day. A safe person skilled in baking the ware can be had for from 40 to 60 cents per diem, and clay washers and mixers at from 20 to 30 cents.

Enamels.—Makers of enamelled copper and porcelain receive much the same wages. The enamelled copper or cloissoné of the present time commands higher prices in the market than any now made elsewhere. There has been the greatest improvement within the last three or four years. When machinery takes the place of the hand in shaping the copper base and in polishing the enamel, the ware can be produced for

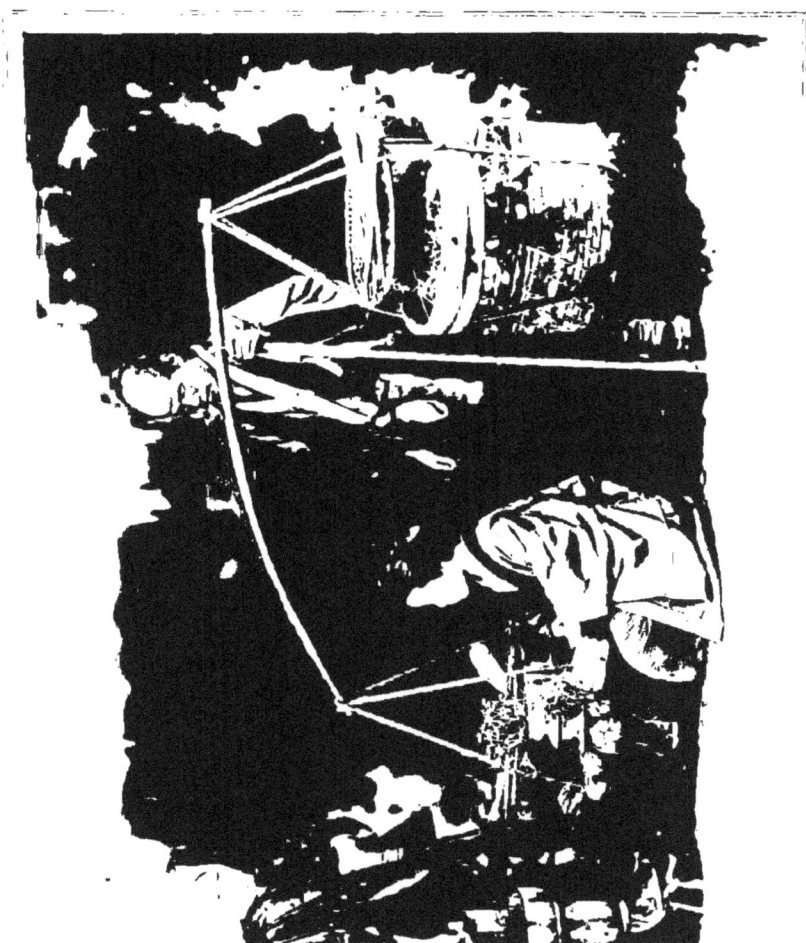

much less than at present, and probably of a superior quality. As it is Japan has no close competitor in the finer articles of this manufacture.

Bronze.—Bronze workers get about the same wages as workers in porcelain. The highest skill in inland bronze manufacture commands from $1 to $1.50 per day, but ordinary skill can be had from 30 to 70 cents per day.

Ivory carvers get from $10 to $20 per month ; carpenters from 25 to 50 cents per day ; blacksmiths are cheaper, and can be had from 18 to 40 cents per diem.

Lacquer.—Modern lacquer workers, in the best product of that art, rank with porcelain and bronze artisans. Wages range from 20 cents to $1.25 per day, according to the skill of the individual and the grade of the article made.

It has been thought the art of making fine lacquer was on the decline, but I think this a mistake, and that as fine, if not finer, articles than ever graced the Tycoon's castle can be made if the same prices are offered.

Ship builders work mostly near the open ports, where wages are much higher than in the interior. A good ship carpenter gets 40 to 50 cents per day, and a foreman from $50 to $60 per month.

PROFESSIONAL LABOR.

As was seen in giving the statistics of education, the average yearly salary of all the school teachers in Japan was 44.72 yen.

Physicians, as a rule, do not charge for the visit to the patient, but for the medicine which they give; but as one who has reputation charges more for the same medicine than the less known practitioner, it amounts to the same thing. An ordinary physician will receive a call in office hours and give medicine for from $12\frac{1}{2}$ to 20 cents. As to charges for surgical cases, the knife was unknown to the old school. The fees of the new foreign school cannot be much higher, for if they were the physicians would not get patronage.

Lawyers.—Until lately there were no native lawyers. Now several are practicing before the courts in Tokio and Yokohama. It can hardly be said that they have established a footing yet, or that the profession has a well-defined existence. As no civil code has been adopted, and as the criminal code has been little modified, it may be a long time before they reach a position of much importance.

Writers, translators, and *interpreters* can be had at all prices, from $10 to $50 per month; *clerks, salesmen,* and *bookkeepers* command from $10 to $20 per month, including board.

COOLY OR COMMON LABOR.

This is the lowest class of labor in Japan. As has been stated, these people were the serfs of the soil. Although the whole class system has been done away with, yet the effect of a thousand years of degradation remains. The year 1868 found this class in utter poverty. Probably not one in a hundred of them owned a foot of land or the rude roof which ill sheltered their heads from the storms. Twelve years have done much to improve their condition. Many now own their own houses and tools. Some have bought land and are now farmers, on their own account. Wages have been raised and schools, in many instances, are available for their children.

Carriers.—Probably the hardest-worked laborers in Japan are the carriers. This class includes the jinrikisha men, carmen, and packers. Jinrikishas, or man-waggons, introduced into Japan by a foreigner, in 1870, are now in use in all parts of the country, and it is estimated that they number between 300,000 and 400,000. A man is expected to go from 30 to 40 miles per day, pull this carriage, of some 50 pounds in weight, with a man weighing 150 more, over all kinds of roads, and he gets from 35 to 60 cents for it. Some own their own jinrikishas, but in most cases a company or guild is the owner, and for rental of a vehicle the cooly must pay from 6 to 10 cents per day. The cost of these carriages is from $12 to $16 each. One of these men will carry you 6 miles in an hour and when you stop to make a call, the poor fellow, bathed in perspiration, waits perhaps, in a cold winter wind or storm, with no protection but his cotton garments. The result is necessarily rheumatism, consumption, and a short life.

Car-men.—There are two kinds of cart carriage— one where the cart is drawn by men, and the other by a bull or cow. Where man-drawn, usually there are four men—two in front and two behind. They draw heavy loads, and go slowly indulging in a sort of measured shout to mark time. In the South, smaller carts are in use—some for two and others for one man. I have seen an old man and a young woman, the latter with a small child strapped on her back, pulling a cart-load of wood or coal up steep hills and over sandy plains. Ten to twelve miles a day with a loaded cart is a day's work, and 600 to 700 pounds an average load for two persons. For this heavy work from 10 to 20 cents per diem is considered good pay.

However dark this picture, these people know how to enjoy it. They go in a train of several carts, taking their food, rain-coats of plaited straw, and sun-hats, and at intervals stop by some stream where there is clear water and cool shade, where, with the laughter and light-heartedness of children, they indulge in their simple meals.

Bull-carts are drawn by only one animal. The driver walks by the latter's side and guides him by a small cord fastened to his nose by an iron ring. The bull is stout, quiet, and gentle ; he will go about 12 to 15 miles per day, and draw 600 to 700 pounds. The earnings of such a cart and man are about 50 cents per day.

Packers.—These are of two kinds—men and women who carry loads of produce and goods on their backs over the mountain paths and along the highways, down to the rivers and sea-coast and those who use horses for the same purpose. Men and women carry from 80 to .

120 pounds each, and go from 12 to 15 miles a day, earning from 10 to 16 cents. The horse, in summer, gets little but grass, with, perhaps, a little rice or barley bran. There are no iron or steel shoes worn by packhorses. They are shod with straw, and in the interior, these straw shoes cost 2 cents per set. On some of the stony roads two sets are required per day.

The other coolie labor has been referred to when treating of farming and mechanical industries, where they are used to do the heavy and coarse work.

FISHERMEN.

Surrounded on all sides by the ocean, indented everywhere by broad gulfs and bays, all the alluvial portions cut up by tidal streams and canals, the waters swarming with a great variety of food-fishes, it is only natural that there should be a numerous fishing population in Japan. There are no separate returns of this class, but it is very large.

Every shore has its fishing villages. All the bays and inlets, on fair days, are white with the sails of fishing-boats. I am inclined to think that this is the lowest class in the country. Their houses are the poorest and dirtiest, and they are the least intelligent. There are fewer schools in these isolated villages then elsewhere and the percentage of illiteracy is greater. Physically they are the equals of the other people, which is owing to a plentiful supply of fish-food. There is no religious or other prejudice against eating fish, and all kinds are cheap.

A good fishing-boat for two men costs about $70. On fair days an average catch is from 60 to 90 cents' worth. The wages of an able-bodied fishermen, working by the day, are 15 to 20 cents. Women and children work along the shores at low-tide, gathering oysters, clams, &c.

The preparation of salted fish gives employment to large numbers of the cheaper class of laborers. This numerous fishing population, the island location of the country, the numbers and variety of fish in all the cheapness of transportation from the fisheries to the centres of population on the seashores and river banks, all have an important bearing upon the welfare of the laboring class.

In the larger towns the fish-markets are all under the control of guilds, and in some places the boats are owned and the men employed by these guilds. In the city of Nagoya, in the province of Owari, the fish guild four years ago owned 1,200 boats and employed 4,000 men. Some of these boats were large and carried 8 and 10 men. Their sales of fish were $1,500,000 per year.

Fish can be had at all prices, from 2 to 12½ cents per pound, according to the quality and the locality where sold. The product of the fisheries in 1878 was about $10,000,000.

MINERS.

The mines of Japan, in the value of the product, do not take high rank. The total value from all mines and quarries 1878 did not exceed $5,000,000.

MUSEME, IN WINTER COSTUME.

Labor is cheap, and for poverty and ignorance the miner takes a position side by side with the fishermen. His lot is harder and his pleasures are less. Common mine labor can be had for from 8 to 20 cents per day, and by the month for less.

Exactly what the mine wealth of Japan is cannot be ascertained at present, and probably will never be known until the country and its hidden resources are opened to foreign skill and enterprise ; and this may be said with equal truth as to the cultivable lands. If worked in large tracts by skilled labor and modern foreign implements, the taxable wealth of the country would be vastly increased.

SPORTS AND PASTIMES.

The national sports and games of Japan were less active and athletic in character than those of Europe and America. The samurai were fond of horseback riding, but the laboring classes were not allowed to ride on the public roads. Even now, when the packhorses are returning unloaded from market and the drivers ride a portion of the way, they make sure to dismount in the presence of any of the old, higher class. The absence of roads also discouraged the practice of equestrianism. Foot races or walking matches were not in vogue. So of boat-racing. Exclusively warlike games and practices were indulged in by the higher classes. They practiced archery and fencing and, on eating and drinking occasions, had trials of strength and skill within doors.

The lower classes had a more active class of sports.

Under the harvest moon you may see a whole village collected to witness wrestling, racing, and fencing. Theatrical performances are popular, and travelling troupes of actors from village to village, erect bamboo and mat shelters, and give entertainments for a week at a time. On such occasions the laboring classes turn out in great numbers, with all their holiday finery on, and enjoy every incident of the performance. Laboring men in the evening go to tea-houses, drink a light wine made from rice, sing songs, play games of skill, and recite in dramatic style from the old historians and poets. Women and girls gossip in groups at some neighbor's house, or at the public baths. Women play a simple game of checkers, while men are skilled in chess. The children have battledore and kite-flying.

In addition to this the Japanese are great travellers. In certain months when farm labor is not pressing 20 or 30 friends and neighbors will arrange a pilgrimage to some of the noted shrines and temples in the mountains, going on foot as far as 150 or 200 miles. They walk leisurely along the roads and paths, talking, laughing and singing. In the middle of the day, when tired, they sleep in the shade of the groves, eat rice and drink tea, and are as happy as the day is long.

These pilgrimages are an important feature in the social life of the laborer. They afford mental and physical relaxation, give extended [observation of wide regions of country, of new, varied, and better industries, and an insight into the life and habits of their far-off countrymen.

There is another amusement to be met with on festival days, which in the smaller villages of the interior, still exerts an influence upon the lower classes. I allude to the wayside story-telling. This afforded the only means which certain classes had of knowing the history of their country. The story-tellers have rude booths, and for a mere pittance recite by the hour the civil and military history of the different dynasties which have ruled the country. They speak the pure old Japanese unmixed with Chinese words, which the learned affected, and thus are perfectly understood by their hearers.

LABOR ORGANIZATIONS.

Every branch of labor and trade has its guild, although not, like those of western countries, originally formed to protect labor from the exactions of capital. The government, for purposes of revenue, farmed out to favorites exclusive privileges of trade or of labor, and these persons formed guilds and levied taxes upon all engaged in such occupations. These organizations, in time, fell more and more under the influence and control of those taxed. They gradually grew to be used for the protection of the interests of the trades. They could petition the local authorities, and, from their numbers and unity, had no inconsiderable influence.

Although the government has abolished this practice of farming these guilds and substituted therefor individual licenses, the guilds still exist and zealously guard the interests of their members.

As has been said, there are no manufactories employing large capital and great numbers of operatives, but the manufactures of Japan are distinctively household. In some cases a few outside laborers are employed but in many, perhaps a majority of these household workshops, the laborer is interested in the capital and profits of the manufacture.

If labor-saving machinery, large capital, and great establishments employing hundreds of people shall ever be introduced, these guilds now operating partially in the interest of labor may assume the importance and influence of the labor organizations in the United States.

FINANCES.

While the finances of a country have an important bearing upon the condition of the laborer, it is not within the province of this paper to enter into an elaborate review of the financial system of this country. Briefly, the estimates of the revenues of the general government are, for the year 1880-'81 $54,558,304. The principal sources of this revenue are as follows :—

1st. Land tax...$41,901,441
2nd. Imports and exports....................... 2,369,462
3rd. Taxes on spirits, tobacco, stamp taxes, licences, &c............................ } 9,000,000
4th. Income from government property, such as sales and rents from public } 1,400,000 lands, yield of mines, &c...............

The burdens of taxation are light upon all industries **except** agriculture, where the tax is a uniform one of 8 per cent. of its value, as has been shown, estimated from its products. The estimated expenditures are the same for the year 1880-'81 as the revenue, the principal items of which are for—

Reduction of national debt	$ 5,817,538
Interest of national debt	15,631,369
Pensions	1,059,403
Expenses of the ten departments of the government	23,051,409
Expenses of local or provincial governments	4,539,280
Police	1,261,500
Miscellaneous : home and foreign industrial exhibitions, libraries, museums, &c.	1,331,559

Currency.—The currency of the country is—

1st.	Treasury notes	$108,683,203
2nd.	National bank notes, about	32,000,000
	Making the total paper circulation about	140,683,203

The treasury notes are irredeemable, but are interchangeable for six per cent. government bonds. There is an annual drawing for a certain amount of these bonds, which are paid at par, in gold.

The national bank issues are secured by a deposit of government bonds of 80 per cent. of the amount so issued, but are redeemable only in treasury notes.

Both the treasury and bank notes are much depreciated and are now, September, 1880, worth from 60 to 70 cents only, in silver.

The debt has been reduced during the past year nearly $11,000,000, and the estimated reduction for the present year is about $6,000,000. The interest on public debt for the present year, 1880-'81, is $15,631,369.

PAUPERISM.

In all time Japan had her beggar class, who were permitted to solicit alms by the roadside, and to live in huts on the waste lands. The origin of this class is unknown. Whether they are descended from the lepers or from pardoned criminals, and thus outcasts, or from the conquered aborigines, is uncertain. Although they may still be seen here and there by the roadsides, the government discourages these proceedings, and in many cases they are arrested and subjected to punishment. There was an attempt some years since, by the various local authorities, to reduce the number of these beggars by furnishing them with labor, food, and clothing, but without marked success. With this exception, the government has never made any provision for the extremely poor. Farms for the poor, pauper asylums, systems of outdoor relief, were and are unknown. In fact, there was little need for them. So little food and clothing will supply the wants of the poor that the near and distant relatives of which the family and class are formed were enabled to provide that little. As the influence of the family organizations grows weaker and their responsibility less, the necessity of some public provision begins to be felt.

There is another feature of society here which makes numbers of aged, indigent people less dependent upon public charity. The family never becomes extinct, the line of descent never ceases. If there are no male children to bear the name, a younger son of another family is adopted, who takes the family name, and upon whom the aged and decrepit lean for support.

THE BLIND.

The number of blind persons in Japan, owing to causes already enumerated, is very large. In every city or village of any size they are organized into associations or guilds, controlled by a president or head man. This officer, although chosen by the members, was formally commissioned by the government authorities. Unless otherwise disabled, the blind are not idle. They go about the streets making their presence known at night by blowing, every few steps, upon a shrill whistle, and are employed as shampooers by any one in pain or suffering from fatigue. Their districts of labor, prices, and general behavior are regulated by the head officer. They live by themselves, do their own cooking, and are in general, a peaceable and worthy class, and not a burden upon the community.

SCENERY.

The remarkable beauty of Japanese scenery has won the admiration of every visitor. Her grand mountain range, covered with trees and shrubs, clothed in perpetual green, towered by the world-renowned Fujiyama, rearing its shining summit above the clouds, reverenced by millions of her people as the reflection of Deity itself, and the holy shrine to which thousands of pilgrims yearly bend their steps; the charming and picturesque valleys, carpeted with richest verdure and blossoming with flowers of a thousand hues, including the lotus, queen of lilies, which fills the atmosphere with its rich perfume; the rushing torrents and winding rivers, sparkling with clearest water; her numerous and varied islands; her indented coasts, bays, and harbors; her varieties of shrubs and trees, and her skies of purest blue—all combine to make their impress on the character of her people.

Cheerfulness of disposition and love of the beautiful are striking characteristics of the natives of Niphon. Born and reared amidst such charms of nature, forms of beauty become to them every-day familiar objects, and it is no matter of wonder that they bring into existence some of the loveliest works of art that human hands have ever formed, or that the smiles of sky and earth, air and sea, should be reflected on their faces and in their lives.

The laborer sings at his toil, goes cheerfully to his simple meal, and engages with the enthusiasm of boyhood in his holiday sports.

ETHNOLOGY.

It is perhaps too early to state with certainty to which of the families of the human race the Japanese belong.

Morton, long since, after examining a number of Japanese crania, decided that they are not of Chinese origin. Their language, which is always considered the strongest evidence of race, makes it certain that they are neither Chinese, Polynesian, or of that aboriginal race to which the inhabitants of north-eastern Asia belong. Whitney and Muller are inclined to place them in the great Indo-European family. If so, the conquerors of these islands must have started from the central

COOLIE, IN WINTER DRESS.

regions of Asia, and instead of travelling west, as the other migratory hordes did, came east, crossed to Japan, and wrested the country from the Ainos, the then possessors of the soil.

ORIENTAL CIVILIZATION.

The distinctive characteristic of Oriental civilization, as compared to ours of the west, is its extreme simplicity of food, dress, houses, household appurtenances, and general style of living. The precepts of religion, the maxims of government, and the fashions of the times inculcate and command the practice of frugality and rigid economy, while the whole influence of western civilization tends to lead the laborer to habits of show and luxury beyond his means. Our style of architecture, of food, and of clothing are incomparably more costly than those of the Orient.

If a Japanese laborer had to live in our style of house, eat our animal flesh and pastries, and wear our clothing, to say nothing of the social demands upon his time and means, the cost of his living would be more than quadrupled, and the price of his products enhanced accordingly. This question of the comparative simplicity and cost of living and of production of the two civilizations will grow in importance as the two systems are brought more and more into contact and competition.

There are seven or eight hundred million of people dwelling on the southern and eastern shores of Asia, the majority of them workers, living up to the requirements of this Oriental simplicity, who are all ready to compete

with our people in every branch of human industry.
And it may be worth our while to inquire if the demands
of our social system do not handicap our laborer too
heavily in the contest. Of course it is not to be con-
templated that our laborers are to be put upon the rice,
fish, or vegetable diet of these eastern workers. Our
climate alone utterly forbids such a consummation, if,
in any view, it were desirable. The labor-saving machinery, created from the active brains of our inventors,
so often looked upon by laboring men as destructive of
employment and ruinous to their interests, constitutes
for the present the barrier which protects them and
their interests against the rapid and perhaps lowering
competition of the vast masses of laborers to which I
have alluded. But this is not all that is needed. The
reduction of taxation and equalization of the burdens
of government, as far as possible, the multiplication
of cheap means of transportation, the building of
economical and comfortable houses in cities, the positve
prevention of swindling in food and clothing, the rigid
scrutiny of all beverages sold, and the prohibition, under
the severest penalties, of the sale of impure drinks, and
the encouragement of proper co-operative associations
for the purchase and sale of good and cheap provisions,
are all necessary for the welfare of our great laboring
population, the producers of our wealth and prosperity.

THOS. B. VAN BUREN,
Consul-General.

United States Consulate-General,
  Kanagawa, October 6th, 1880.

TABLE A.—SHOWING PRICES OF FOOD IN JAPAN, ACCORDING TO QUALITY.

		CENTS.		
Rice	per pound	2	to	3
Barley	per pound	1¼	to	2
Wheat	per pound	1	to	1¾
Millet	per pound	¾	to	1
Wheat flour	per pound	2	to	3
Salt	per pound	½	to	¾
Sugar, common brown	per pound	4	to	5
Sugar, white brown	per pound	8	to	10
Peas	per pound	1½	to	2
Beans	per pound	1½	to	2
Potatoes, Irish	per 100 pounds	20	to	40
Potatoes, sweet	per 100 pounds	12	to	25
Onions	per 100 pounds	20	to	40
Carrots	per 100 pounds	20	to	30
Cabbages	per 100 pounds	15	to	20
Egg plants	per pound	1	to	1½
Parsnips	per 100 pounds	20	to	30
Turnips	per 100 pounds	10	to	20
Squashes	per 100 pounds	11	to	15
Watermelon	each	2	to	5
Muskmelons	each	1	to	1½
Peaches	per pound	2	to	3
Pears	per pound	1	to	2
Plums	per pound	2	to	3
Grapes	per pound	2	to	2½
Ducks, tame	each	20	to	35
Ducks, wild	each	15	to	30
Geese, tame	each	40	to	80

TABLE A.—SHOWING PRICES OF FOOD IN JAPAN, ACCORDING

TO QUALITY.—*Continued.*

			CENTS.		
Geese, wild	each	30	to	50
Pigeons	each	10	to	12
Pheasants	each	10	to	20
Fresh fish	per pound	2	to	20
Oysters	per quart	6	to	10
Clams	per quart	6	to	10
Salt fish	per pound	3	to	10
Beef	per pound	12	to	18
Pork	per pound	10	to	15

As I have remarked, little animal flesh is eaten by the laborer. It is only in the open ports that it is at all used.

Milk, butter, and cheese are also unknown articles of food.

TABLE B.—JAPANESE TAXATION.

Land tax (local and government), 3 per cent. on valuation.

Corporations :

On sales amounting to—	YEN.	SEN.
10,000 yen and over	15	00
7,000 to 10,000 yen	13	00
5,000 to 7,000 yen	10	00
3,000 to 5,000 yen	7	00
1,000 to 3,000 yen	5	00
700 to 1,000 yen	3	00
Under 700 yen	1	50

Merchants, wholesale :

On sales amounting to—	YEN.	SEN.
10,000 yen and over	15	00
7,000 to 10,000 yen	13	00
5,000 to 7,000 yen	10	00
3,000 to 5,000 yen	7	00
1,000 to 3,000 yen	5	00
700 to 1,000 yen	3	00
500 to 700 yen	2	00
300 to 500 yen	1	00
100 to 300 yen		50
Under 100 yen		25

Merchants, retail, and goods brokers :

On sales amounting to—		
10,000 yen and over	15	00
7,000 to 10,000 yen	13	00
5,000 to 7,000 yen	10	00
3,000 to 5,000 yen	7	00
1,000 to 3,000 yen	5	00
700 to 1,000 yen	3	00
500 to 700 yen	2	00
300 to 500 yen	1	00
100 to 300 yen		5
30 to 100 yen		2.5

Public and private libraries, lenders of furniture and articles of clothing, &c. :

On gross income.............................1 per cent.

Commission merchants :

On gross commissions received...........$1\frac{1}{2}$ per cent.

Contractors :

On gross receipts.............................$1\frac{1}{2}$ per cent.

Manufacturers, corporations :

On sales amounting to—	YEN.	SEN.
10,000 yen and over	15	00
7,000 to 10,000 yen	13	00
5,000 to 7,000 yen	10	00
3,000 to 5,000 yen	5	00
1,000 to 3,000 yen	3	00
700 to 1,000 yen	2	00
500 to 700 yen	1	00
300 to 500 yen		50
Under 300 yen		25

Mechanics :

House-painters, clock, paper, and lacquer-ware makers, carvers, image-makers, photographers, pen-makers, picture-painters, match manufacturers, makers and mixers of colors, embroiderers, tailors, washmen, gold, silver and tin smiths, pot and kettle workers, blacksmiths, carpenters, locksmiths, porcelain and bronze workers. Same as above.

Carriers :

Carriages—	YEN.
2 horse carts per annum	3
1 horse cart per annum	2
Jinrikishas to carry two persons	2
Jinrikishas to carry one person	1
Wheelbarrows	1
Pack-horses	1
Man-carts, two men	1
Man-carts, four men	2

Auctioneers :
  On gross sales........................... 3 to 5 per cent.

Theatrical, acrobatic, and other exhibitions :
  In houses, on gross receipts................. 5 per cent.

Billiard-rooms, bowling-alleys, archery, galleries: YEN. SEN.
  Per month........... 1   00

Eating-houses :
  On gross receipts of—   YEN.   SEN.
    800 yen and over..................... 12   00
    From 500 to 800 yen 10   00
    From 300 to 500 yen 6   00
    From 200 to 300 yen 3   00
    200 yen and under............................ 1   50

Hotels, with stables attached :
  On receipts of—
    800 yen and over, per annum 10   00
    500 to 800 yen per annum..................... 9   00
    300 to 500 yen per annum.................. ... 7   00
    200 to 300 yen per annum..................... 2   50
    100 to 200 yen per annum 1   00
    Under 100 yen per annum   50

Eating-houses, in each of which only one kind of food is
    permitted to be served :

  On gross receipts of—   YEN.   SEN.
    800 yen and over, per annum..................10   00
    500 to 800 yen per annum..................... 7   50
    300 to 500 yen per annum..................... 5   00
    200 to 300 yen per annum..................... 2   50
    100 to 200 yen per annum.............,........ 1   00
    Under 100 yen per annum....................   50

Pawn-shops :

On gross receipts of—   YEN.   SEN.

    10,000 yen and over 15   00

    7,000 to 10,000 yen.............................13   00

    5,000 to 7,000 yen.............................10   00

    3,000 to 5,000 yen............................ 7   00

    1,000 to 3,000 yen............................. 5   00

    700 to 1,000 yen............................ 3   00

    500 to   700 yen............................ 2   00

    300 to   500 yen............................ 1   00

    100 to   300 yen...........................   50

    Under 100 yen...........................   25

Exchange brokers :

    On income, same as above.

Transportation companies :

    On gross earnings of, same as above.

Junk-shops :

On transactions of—

    5,000 yen and over 10   00

    3,000 to 5,000 yen.............................. 9   00

    1,000 to 3,000 yen.............................. 7   00

    700 to 1,000 yen.............................. 5   00

    500 to   700 yen.............................. 3   00

    300 to   500 yen.............................. 2   00

    Under 300 yen.............................. 1   00

Booths (for tea drinking) :

    Per month, each..................................   50

Places for sale of ice-water :

    Per month, each..................................   80

Bath houses :
    On gross receipts........................... 1 per cent.

Barbers' license :
    Two yen per year, and 1 per cent. of gross receipts.

Intelligence offices :
    License of 5 yen per year.

Dancing-masters, music-teachers, street story-tellers & actors :
    License, 1. yen per month.
Wrestlers :
    License of 50 sen per month.

Regular singing and dancing girls :
    License from 1.50 to 3.50 yen per month.

Licensed attendants upon dancing and singing entertainments:
    Seventy-five sen to 2 yen per month.

Water-power mills for hulling rice :	YEN.	SEN.
20 stamps and over, per annum...............	5	00
10 to 20 stamps per annum......................	3	00
5 to 10 stamps per annum.....................	1	50
3 to 5 stamps per annum..		50
Less than 3 stamps per annum...............		30

Live stock :		
Horses, each, per annum........................	1	00
Grown cattle, each, per annum...............		20
Young cattle, each, per annum................		10
Sheep and hogs, each, per annum...........		5

Marine licenses :		
Junks or native vessels, with a capacity to carry 500 bushels and under, per annum...	1	00

Every 500 bushels additional, per annum... 1   00

Steamers, each 100 tons measurement, per annum.................................. } 15   00

Sailing vessels, foreign model, each 100 tons, per annum........................... } 10   00

Small boats, 20 sen to 1 yen per annum, according to size.

Shooting licenses :
Professional hunters, per annum............. 1   20
Others, per annum...............................10   00

Horse and cattle dealers :
Licenses, per annum............................. 2   00
For every animal sold, additional per annum 1   00

Manufacturers of weights and measures :
Twenty-five per cent. ad valorem.

Druggists :
Licenses, 2 yen per annum.
All patent medicines, 25 per cent. ad valorem.

Manufacturers of alcoholic drinks :
The tax is levied upon the quantity of rice used in brewing.
Common saké (a species of wine), from 2 to 4 yen, according to quality, upon each koku (about 5 bushels) of rice used.

Tobacco :   YEN.
License, wholesale dealers, per annum...............10
License, retail dealers, per annum..................... 5
There is also a stamp tax of 2 per cent. on all sales.

Stamped paper :
All written transactions of 10 yen and above pay a tax of 3 sen.
No agreement in writing can be enforced without a stamp.

Copyright :

The price of 6 copies of the work is charged.

Stock-brokers :

Ten per cent. of commissions.

Bankers :

On every 1,000 yen loaned, 7 yen.

Passengers on foreign vessels, 10 sen per head.

Houses of prostitution, 1 to 7 yen per month.

Every inmate, 1 to 4 yen per month.

Taxes are collected in the different Fu and Ken (provinces of the Empire), and the expenditures for local purposes must first be approved by the general government.

Note.—The statistics in this report, relating to agricultural production, it will be perceived were taken from returns of some years ago. Later tables are now available, and in many instances show a marked increase. The local land-tax was, as above stated, limited to ½ per cent., but I have since learned that in this Ken of Kanagawa the local land-tax has been increased to about 2½ per cent., making a total land-tax of 5 per cent. As far as my information extends a like additional tax is imposed in all the Fu and Ken of the Empire, varying in amount according to local requirements.

T. B. V. B.

[To this report a series of maps, coloured to show the relative population, and growth of the various cereals, &c., of great value to the student of the important matters dealt with, is appended; but, of course, they cannot be introduced here.—Publisher.]

POTTERY AND PORCELAIN INDUSTRIES

OF

J A P A N.

—◦—

REPORT

OF

CONSUL-GENERAL VAN BUREN,

OF KANAGAWA.

OUR knowledge of Japanese pottery dates from the return of the adventurous Portuguese navigators who, under Vasco da Gama, first visited the East in the latter part of the fifteenth century. Upon their return they brought the first specimens of white translucent porcelain ever seen in Europe.* It was known as "Indian siggillata," and consisted of specimens of Chinese and Japanese blue and white ware. This was more than two centuries before Bottcher made the first pieces of true porcelain produced in Europe.

During the sixteenth, seventeenth, and eighteenth centuries glimpses of this Japanese art were seen through the Portuguese and Dutch intercourse with Japan, but

---

* See the note on the following page.

it was not until after Japan, was open to foreign trade, in the middle of the nineteenth century, that opportunities for a thorough study were afforded.

Japanese chronicles claim that the first pottery was made in the year 660 B.C., but if we accept the testimony of the "shell heaps or mounds" it has a much earlier date than that.

It was not, however, until the Christian era that the art made any considerable advances. It is recorded that the potter's wheel was not introduced till the year 724, A.D.

In the year 1223, A.D., great improvements in the manufacture and decoration of ware were made. From that date to the sixteenth century the great potteries of Owari, Hizen, Mino, Kioto, Kaga, and Satsuma were established.

The Raku-Yaki or crackled ware was first made in Kioto at the commencement of the sixteenth century. The best old Hizen ware, that which is still the most admired, was made in Arita, Hizen, in 1580 to 1585.* The old Satsuma dates from 1592.

Porcelain clays are found in nearly all portions of

---

* Since the first publication of the foregoing report, my attention has been called by the accomplished editor of the *Japan Mail* to certain errors in dates into which I have fallen by following too literally some writers upon old porcelain who have unwittin ly confounded fine porcelain with pottery. From further study of the subject I am convinced that the pieces of "Chinese ware" at it was then called carried to Europe by Vasco da Gama in 1499, were Chinese, and if any Japanese specimens were included they were of pottery and not fine porcelain. Excellence in porcelain, I am satisfied was not attained in Japan until the middle or latter part of the 17th century instead of towards the close of the 16th century as stated by me.

the country, and, what is of great economic advantage, the different kinds are usually found in close proximity and of the purest and best quality, and in many places near water transportation. I believe in all cases every variety of clay used in the manufacture of pottery is found in a natural state. There is no necessity to manufacture the quartzose or fusible clays as is done in other parts of the world and which adds much to the cost of the ware. It is still more remarkable to find one clay that contains both the fusible and infusible materials in such proportions as to make a light, beautiful, translucent, durable porcelain. I am not aware that such clays are found in any other country. The beautiful egg-shell ware from Nagasaki, so much admired, is so made, and there are other localities where such clays are found and worked.

In order that the chemical composition of porcelain clays may be understood, I give the formula of a mineral found by Johnson & Blake in true porcelain clay or kaolin, which is as follows :—

Per cent. of silica.................................... 46.33
Per cent. of alumina 39.77
Per cent. of water 13.9

It is to this mineral that the peculiar plasticity of clays is due. The silica is the fusible and the alumina the infusible element of the clay. In proportion as the silica predominates the ware will be nitreous, translucent, light, and brittle, and in the same proportion as the alumina predominates the ware will have weight, opacity, and tenacity, or cohesion.

It must be borne in mind that only opaque, heavy porcelain is made from kaolin, or clay, in which the silica is only from 30 to 40 per cent. of the whole. The fine translucent ware is made by the addition of petunse, a quartzose clay. Petunse is a highly silicious clay resulting from the decomposition of quartzose granite. These two are mixed according to the ware to be made. I believe that natural petunse is not found in Europe or America, but that an artificial quartzose mixture is made to take its place. The two clays, kaolin and petunse, are mixed for common porcelain in the proportion of two parts of kaolin to one part petunse. The biscuit made from this combination will contain from 50 to 60 per cent. of silica and 30 to 40 per cent. of alumina, the remainder being composed of water, soda, potash, magnesia, &c. In the lighter highly translucent ware more petunse and less kaolin is used. In the best ware the biscuit, so mixed, will contain from 75 to 80 per cent. of silicious or fusible matter and from 15 to 18 per cent. of alumina or infusible matter.

In several localities in Japan a single clay, as I have said, contains these materials in the exact proportions required for the various kinds of porcelain.

At Arita, in Hizen, they have a clay that contains 78¾ per cent. of silica and 17¾ per cent. of alumina. From this clay they make the delicate translucent egg-shell ware without the addition of any other matter· From an adjoining bluff they take a clay that has 50 per cent. of silica and 38 per cent. of alumina. From this common porcelain is made.

SATSUMA VASE,

(IN POSSESSION OF THE WRITER.)

Nature seems to have mixed these fusible and infusible materials ready for the potter's hands in all the various proportions which he requires for all grades of pottery, from the dark opaque earthen ware to the light translucent egg-shell porcelain; and I repeat that I do not know of any other country where the potter is so favored.

The abundance and general distribution of potter's clay over the whole area of the Japanese Islands is best shown by the following statement of the number of places it is found in in the different provinces :—

	No. of Places.
Province of Yamashiro	15
Province of Hoki	15
Province of Suwo	3
Province of Iyo	18
Province of Hizen	30
Province of Higo	30
Province of Owari	20
Province of Mikawa	56
Province of Idzu	15
Province of Musashi	12
Province of Mino	26

In the whole of Japan there are 283 localities where this clay is deposited. Of course many of these furnish only inferior clays, but they are all fitted for use in some of the various kinds of pottery.

These clays are thoroughly powdered by means of what are called " balance pounders," run in some localities by water-power, but the work is often done by hand. The powder is then decanted, dried, and stored away in cake form on boards or in flat boxes. This dough does not go through the process of fermentation, as with the English dough in Staffordshire.

The shaping is almost exclusively done on the potter's wheel, which is set on a pivot working in a porcelain eye. Ordinarilfy the potter turns his own wheel, but in Hizen it is kept in motion by means of a band connected with its pivot and another wheel turned by a boy.

In making dishes of other shapes than round, a crude mold is sometimes used.

After the clay has been shaped on the wheel it is set away for drying. Usually in two or three days it is considered sufficiently dry for smoothing, which is done on the wheel with a sharp curved knife.

The material is now made into " bisque," or biscuit, by a preliminary baking in small ovens, when it is ready for painting if it is to be painted on the biscuit; if not, it is ready for the glazing. In either event it will then go to the large furnaces for the final baking. The kilns for this purpose are always built on hill-sides, and are connected together, increasing in size from the lower to the higher ones, and in number from 4 to 25. These kilns are so constructed that the draft is from the lowest one, in addition to which each kiln has its own firing place. The result of this construction is that the upper ones are much the most intensely heated, and the ware is arranged accordingly; that which requires the least baking in the lower kiln, and so on. These connecting kilns have the merit of being heat-saving, but they are usually small and badly constructed, and the heat in none of them is uniform.

The glaze is made from the silicious clay and potash

extracted from wood-ashes. This potash is not a pure white, which accounts for the usual dirty color of un-painted Japanese ware.

The painting varies in the different districts. In Owari the greater portion of the ware is painted a cobalt blue. The cobalt ore is found in the bluffs near the clay deposits, and is used to paint the cheaper wares. Some German cobalt is used. The best comes from China. The painting with cobalt is done on the biscuit before glazing.

A very handsome ware is now being made in several districts, and painted on the glaze. For this kind of painting the colors are mixed with a silicate of lead and potash and baked the third time in a small furnace at a low temperature.

The coloring oxides in use are those of copper, cobalt, iron, antimony, manganese, and gold. These are used unfluxed by the painter, and are baked in a temperature which fluxes and produces the desired colors.

Some critic has divided all Japanese porcelain paint-ing into two classes—decorative and graphic. The first is used only to improve the appearance of the vessel upon which it is placed. This class includes all the ware except that of the province of Kaga, which was classed as graphic or delineative, and shows all the trades, occupations, sports, customs, and costumes of the people, as well as the scenery, flora, and fauna of the country. I believe he is substantially correct.

It is not within the scope of a paper of this kind to describe all the pottery of the many districts of Japan.

I shall, however, allude briefly to some of the principal kinds.

"Owari" ware is made in the old province of that name. It is not as translucent but stronger and more tenacious than some of the Hizen manufacture. The principal potteries are at a village called Sèto, 12 miles from the sea. In this village there are more than 200 kilns. The ware is mostly painted a cobalt blue; the best, as before remarked, being done with Chinese cobalt. Some of this blue and white ware is very beautiful, and I believe is more and more fancied by foreigners. The painting is merely decorative, and consists of branches of trees, grass, flowers, birds, and insects. All these the artist copies from nature with a skill unequaled by any other people. Within the few past years white ware in foreign styles and shapes has been made and painted in blue, green, and gold. All the Owari ware is true hard-paste porcelain, and is strong and durable.

In Hizen a number of wares are manufactured. The kind known as "Imari" is made at a place called Arita, but painted at Imari. The colors in use are red, blue, green, and gold. These are combined in various pro. portions, but as a rule the red predominates. Generally the surface of the vessel is divided into medallions or figures which alternately have red, blue, or white background, with figures in green or blue and gold. It is certainly a strikingly beautiful ware.

The egg-shell porcelain sold at Nagasaki is made in this province from Arita clay. As I have said

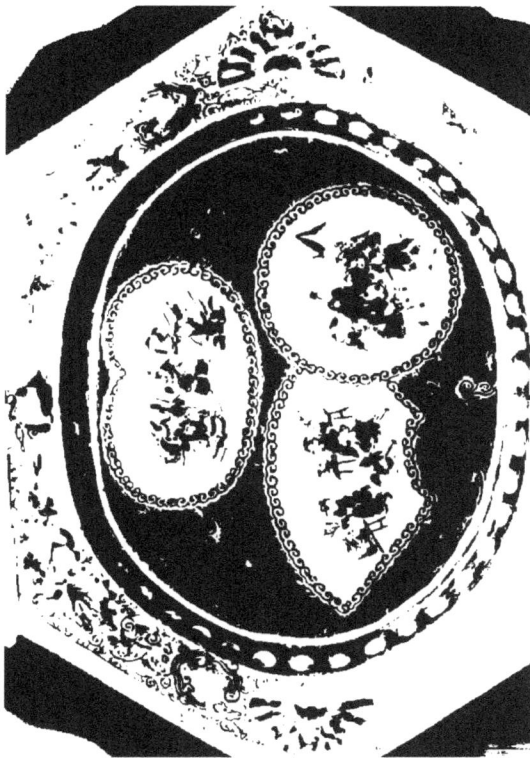

in speaking of clays, this ware is made from clay with no admixture of fusible matter except what the clay contains naturally.

The province of Satsuma is noted for crackled ware. It cannot be classed as a true porcelain, or rather it is a soft paste porcelain. The old ware was confined to small vessels, but in later years some large vases have been made. The glaze is a silicate of alumina and potash, and the best ware has a complete net-work of the finest crackles. The painting is of birds and flowers, and noted for its delicate lines of green, red, and gold.

The "Kioto" ware is much like the Satsuma in color and crackle, but is lighter and more porous. The decorations are also much like the Satsuma ware, being of birds and flowers.

There is a kind of ware made in Kioto called yeraku, the whole body of which is covered with a red oxide of iron, and then over this mythical figures in gold are traced.

The "Kaga" ware is faience, and in the style of painting is unlike any other in Japan. The predominating color is a light sesquioxide of iron red used with green and gold. The designs with which it is profusely decorated are trees, grasses, flowers, birds, and figures of all classes of people, with their costumes, occupations, and pastimes, and hence the painting has been called the graphic or delineation style.

The "Banko" ware is made in the country at the head of the Owari Bay. It is an unglazed stone ware, very light and durable, made on molds in irregular shapes and decorated with figures in relief.

On the island of Awadji a delicate, creamy, crackled, soft-paste porcelain is made. The figures used in decoration are birds and flowers, but outlined by heavy dark lines.

There are several varieties of wares made in different parts of the country with glazings of different colors, including various shades of blue, green, yellow, and red. Some of these are exceedingly beautiful.

Besides these few principal manufactures of which I have given an outline, a large number of other kinds of pottery are produced in Japan, and some new styles are being brought into notice.

This important industry has been greatly stimulated by the foreign demand and by the success of Japanese exhibitors at the exhibitions at Vienna, Paris, and Philadelphia.

The great variety and excellence of Japanese clays, the proximity of their location to the sea, the cheapness of labor, and the beauty and originality of their decorations should, at no distant day, make Japan one of the foremost competitors in the porcelain markets of the world.

THOS. B. VAN BUREN,
Consul-General.

UNITED STATES CONSULATE-GENERAL,
Kanagawa, Japan, January 6th, 1881.

www.ingramcontent.com/pod-product-compliance
Lightning Source LLC
Chambersburg PA
CBHW03235828 0326
41935CB00008B/614